Flavorful Destinations

Traveling the World
Through Food and Drink

Cindy & Jack Luce and Tracy & Chris Baker

Contents

About Us

We love to travel, and we love to cook! *Flavorful Destinations* captures both those interests and will take you around the world through food and drink. You won't have to leave your home.

Since 2020, we have created menus for over 50 countries, regions, and states and prepared the complete meals. As there are 195 countries in the world, plus states and provinces, we may need more than one edition of *Flavorful Destinations*.

The idea for *Flavorful Destinations* originated as a way to entertain ourselves during COVID-19. It was recommended during COVID-19 that people isolate themselves, but they could and did form small groups for socialization. We formed our own "bubble." Since we live next door to each other, getting together weekly was convenient and simple for the four of us.

Our first 17 weekly get-togethers featured only cocktails and desserts. Here are a few examples: Pisco Sours and Passion Fruit Mousse from Peru; Mojitos and Rum Cake from Cuba; Margaritas and Mexican Tea Cakes from Mexico;

Chunky Monkey and Brigadeiro from Brazil; Tequila Sunrise and Arizona Sunshine Pie from Arizona; Swamp Water and Key Lime Pie from Florida; Manhattans and New York Cheesecake from New York; and Amarula and Malva Pudding from Africa.

We evolved into having full dinners complete with cocktails, appetizers, soup or salad, entrees, side dishes, and desserts. Each couple would select a country, state or region, research and plan an authentic menu, order supplies and prepare and serve the meal.

Grants Pass, Oregon, has a population of approximately 36,000 people. Our small city did not always have the specialty ingredients we needed to prepare ethnic foods. However, we did discover sources in Grants Pass that we had not otherwise known of or frequented such as The Herb Shop on G Street or Gooseberries on Redwood Avenue. Sometimes we made the trip to Medford (40 miles away) to shop at Trader Joe's, local Asian or Mexican markets, or we ordered items on Amazon.

The Bakers served our first official dinner on our 18th week together of COVID-19 isolation. Chris and Tracy featured French 75 cocktails, French Champagne, assorted French cheeses, Beef Bourguignon and Yogurt Cake topped with Blueberry Compote. It was the beginning of many meals of interest and excellence!

After each dinner, we would watch a YouTube travel video or two featuring the country of the week. (Frequently, the Bakers had us watch "The Booze Traveler" featuring Jack Maxwell. Jack Maxwell is the Anthony Bourdain of the beverage world.) In this way, we learned about the geography of the country, places most visited, food, traditions, beverages, culture, history and more.

The pandemic brought challenges for dining together. In the beginning, we ate outside. Each couple occupied a table six or more feet apart from the other table. As the weather cooled, and we went inside, we still sat separately and distanced ourselves. There were not any communal bowls for appetizers, bread or rolls. When an appetizer was served, it was put on a separate plate for each diner by the cook of the evening. We scrubbed, wiped and sanitized all surfaces. As we moved around the living room and dining room, each person kept an appropriate distance from the others.

We are adventurous eaters. Jack and I have eaten dried mopane worms in Africa, whitebait on white bread in New Zealand, hundred-year-old eggs and chicken feet in China, and guinea pigs in Peru. Chris and Tracy are seafood aficionados and love to feast upon calamari, mussels, octopus, clams, scallops, oysters, tuna, salmon, shrimp and lobster. Our featured menus and recipes do not, for the most part, feature exotic foodstuffs. Our research led us to "typical" or traditional meals in each country.

Nowadays many people are gluten-free, vegan, or vegetarian. Our cookbook is not designed for restricted diets. It is designed for adventurous people who are interested in seeking to expand their palettes with a dash of culture and history thrown in.

You will note that some of the items listed in the menus do not have recipes. For example, we served rye bread with our Icelandic meal. Rye bread is available at a supermarket, so it was our opinion that a recipe was not needed.

It has been so much fun creating and researching the menus, finding the ingredients, and preparing and serving the food. This project helped us survive the isolation and boredom of the pandemic.

We continue to celebrate travel, food, and our readers!

Bon Appétit!

BELIZE

MENU

Rum Punch
Jicama and Mango Salad
Stewed Chicken
Potato Salad
Stewed Beans
Bread Pudding

Interesting Belizean facts:

1. Belize has the second largest barrier reef in the world.
2. About 40% of Belize is either a marine reserve, national park, or wildlife sanctuary.
3. The Belize Blue Hole is one of the deepest ocean sink holes in the world.

RECIPES

RUM PUNCH
6 Servings

2 cups white rum
1 cup of coconut rum
2 1/2 cups orange juice

2 1/2 cups pineapple juice
1/2 cup fresh lime juice
3 tbsp. grenadine

1. Place rum in large pitcher or punch bowl.
2. Add orange juice and pineapple juice.
3. Mix in fresh lime juice and grenadine. Add enough grenadine to make the punch a pretty pink.
4. Stir ingredients and pour into short rocks glasses filled with ice.
5. Garnish with slices of orange.

JICAMA and MANGO SALAD
6 Servings

1 medium jicama
2 small cucumbers
3 medium mangoes

1/4 cup roughly chopped cilantro leaves
2 tsp. powdered dried chili
2 limes, juiced
Salt

1. Peel and cut the jicama into long thin strips.
2. Slice the cucumbers in half, scoop out the seeds and then cut into strips similar in size to the jicama strips.
3. Cut mangoes into wedges.
4. Place the jicama, cucumbers, and mangoes in a large bowl. Add the cilantro, powdered chili and lime juice. Season with salt to taste.
5. Garnish with cilantro sprigs.

STEWED CHICKEN
6 Servings

Whole chicken, cut into pieces
10 cloves garlic minced
1 tbsp. Maggi chicken bouillon seasoning - or bouillon of your choice
1 tsp. thyme, fresh
2 tbsp. Sazonador Total by Goya or salt and pepper
7 tbsp. olive oil, divided
1 tsp. brown sugar
3 tbsp. Belize Recado Rojo or Achiote Rojo, divided
1 qt. chicken broth – unsalted or low sodium preferred, may not use all of it
1 onion, diced
1 green bell pepper, diced

1 small bunch of cilantro, chopped
Salt and pepper, to taste

1. Mix the garlic, chicken bouillon, thyme, Sazonador, 4 tbsp. of olive oil, and 2 tbsp. of Recado Rojo in a small bowl to make the marinade.
2. Season the chicken all over with the marinade, and refrigerate at least one hour, but preferably overnight.
3. Heat 3 tbsp. of olive oil in a cast iron or other type of heavy pan over medium-high heat; mix in the brown sugar. When hot, fry the chicken until all sides are golden brown. If your pan is not big enough for all of the chicken to lay flat, fry in bunches.
4. Place the cooked chicken in a large saucepan and add just enough chicken broth to cover the chicken. Add the green pepper, onion, and 1 tbsp. of Recado Rojo and mix well.
5. Bring to a boil, then reduce to a simmer.
6. Cover and simmer for 45 minutes to one hour. Remove the cover the last 15 minutes to reduce the sauce.
7. Salt and pepper to taste. Sprinkle with cilantro before serving.

POTATO SALAD
6 Servings

6 medium Yukon Gold potatoes   3 tbsp. dill pickle juice
4 hard boiled eggs, diced   3/4 cup mayonnaise
1 small sweet onion, diced   1 - 2 tbsp. yellow mustard
3 dill pickles, diced

1. Place the potatoes in a large pot of cold, salted water and bring to a boil. Reduce heat to a lightly rolling boil. Cook for 20-25 minutes or until the potatoes are tender. Drain and set aside to cool.
2. Peel the skins from the potatoes and cut into chunks. Place potatoes in a large bowl. Add the eggs, onion, and dill pickles. Mix well.
3. In a small bowl mix the mayonnaise, pickle juice, and mustard. Pour over the potato mixture and mix well. Salt and pepper, to taste.
4. Refrigerate for at least one hour or overnight before serving.

STEWED BEANS
8 Servings

1 lb. dried red kidney beans
1 tbsp. olive oil
1 onion, diced
10 cloves garlic, minced
1 ham hock

2 qts. chicken broth
2 bay leaves
1 tbsp. Sazonador Total by Goya
1 bunch cilantro, chopped
Salt, to taste

1. Heat olive oil on medium high in a large pot. Add minced garlic and onion; cook stirring constantly for around 3 minutes.
2. Add beans, ham hock, Sazonador Total, bay leaves, and chicken broth to the garlic and onion. Add enough chicken broth to cover the beans by about two inches. If not enough chicken broth to cover beans, add water to cover beans.
3. Bring to a boil, then reduce and simmer for 1.5 hours. Check periodically to see if beans are still covered with chicken broth; if not add more chicken broth or water to cover.
4. When beans have cooked about 1.5 hours, check for tenderness. If not tender, continue cooking. When tender, add the cilantro and stir. Salt to taste.
5. Sprinkle a small amount of cilantro on the top to garnish.

BREAD PUDDING
12 Servings

3 cans of condensed milk
3 cans of evaporated milk
1 tsp. lemon extract

5 eggs
1 loaf of white bread

1. Preheat oven to 350 degrees.
2. In a large bowl, combine the condensed milk, evaporated milk, lemon extract, and eggs. Whisk until smooth and well blended.
3. Cut the bread into 1 inch cubes and place them in a large, shallow baking dish (9 x 13 inch).
4. Pour the liquid mixture over the bread ensuring all pieces are fully coated. Gently press down any uncoated bread. Allow the mixture to sit for 20 minutes to absorb the milk mixture.
5. Bake for 1 hour 20 minutes. Halfway through cooking, poke several holes with a knife to ensure even cooking.
6. Remove from oven and let cool slightly. Cut into squares and serve warm with a scoop of vanilla ice cream.

CHINA

MENU

Tsingtao
Green Tea
Wonton Soup
Sweet and Sour Chicken
Roasted Duck with Plum Sauce
Garlic Bok Choy
Sticky Rice
Green Tea Ice Cream

Interesting Chinese Facts:

1. The Terracotta Army was discovered by farmers in 1974.
2. The Chinese New Year celebration lasts for 15 days.
3. Tiananmen Square contains the Mausoleum of Mao Zedong.

WONTON SOUP

4 servings

2/3 lb. ground pork
2 tsp. soy sauce
2 tsp. chives, thinly sliced
1 tsp. rice wine vinegar
1 tsp. cornstarch
1 tsp. grated ginger
1 clove garlic, minced
1/2 tsp. crushed red pepper flakes
1/2 tsp. sesame oil
1 package square wonton wrappers
1/4 cup water

FOR THE SOUP

8 cups chicken broth
2" piece of peeled ginger
2 tsp. soy sauce
2 cloves garlic, minced
1/4 tsp. sesame oil
2 tbsp. sliced green onions, for garnish

1. In a large bowl, mix pork, soy sauce, chives, vinegar, corn-starch, ginger, garlic, red pepper flakes and sesame oil until incorporated.
2. Using your finger, wet the edges of wonton wrapper with water. Place half a tablespoon of pork filling in the center of the wonton wrapper. Fold wonton in half diagonally to create a triangle and seal the edges. Fold the two identical corners in on each other and press again to seal. Repeat until all wonton wrappers are filled.
3. Bring all soup ingredients to a boil. Simmer on low for 10 minutes, then remove ginger and bring it back to a boil. Lower in wontons and cook for 10 minutes more. Serve into bowls immediately and garnish with green onions.

SWEET AND SOUR CHICKEN

4 servings

1 lb. skinless, boneless chicken
  breasts, cut into 1- inch chunks
1 large egg white
1/2 tsp. salt
2 tsp. cornstarch
1 can pineapple chunks (10 oz.),
  drained, juice reserved
1/4 cup juice from the
  canned pineapple
1/4 cup white vinegar
1/4 cup ketchup
3 tbsp. brown sugar
1 tbsp. plus 1 tsp.
  vegetable oil
1 red bell pepper, cut into
  1-inch chunks
1 yellow bell pepper, cut into
  1-inch chunks
1 tsp. grated fresh ginger
1/2 tsp. salt

1. In a bowl, combine the chicken with the egg white, salt and cornstarch. Stir to coat the chicken evenly. Let sit for 15 minutes at room temperature or up to overnight in the refrigerator.
2. Whisk together the pineapple juice, vinegar, ketchup, salt and brown sugar to create the sweet and sour sauce.
3. Heat a large frying pan over high heat until a bead of water instantly sizzles and evaporates. Pour in 1 tbsp. of vegetable oil and swirl to coat. It's important that the pan is very hot. Add the chicken and spread the pieces out in one layer. Let the chicken fry, untouched for 1 minute, until the bottoms are browned. Flip and fry the other side for 1 minute. The chicken should still be pinkish in the middle. Dish out the chicken onto a clean plate, leaving as much oil in the pan as possible.
4. Reduce the heat to medium and add the remaining 1 tsp. of vegetable oil. Let the oil heat up before adding the red and yellow bell pepper chunks and ginger. Fry for 1 minute.
5. Add the pineapple chunks and the sweet and sour sauce. Turn up the heat to high. When the sauce is simmering, add the chicken pieces back in.
6. Let simmer for 1 to 2 minutes, until the chicken is cooked through. Timing depends on how thick you've cut your chicken. The best way to tell if the chicken is done is to take a piece out and cut into it. If it's pink, add another minute to the cooking time.
7. Taste the sauce and add more brown sugar or vinegar to suit your taste.

ROASTED DUCK with Plum Sauce
8 servings

1 whole duck (5 to 6 lbs.) defrosted	1 tsp. paprika
Boiling water	1 orange, cut into quarters
1 tbsp. salt	4 cloves garlic, minced
1 1/2 tsp. black pepper	2 stalks celery, cut into 2" pieces
	1 jar Plum Sauce

1. Make sure the duck is thoroughly defrosted. Start a large pot of water (deep enough to submerge a whole duck) on the stove, bringing to a rolling boil. Preheat oven to 425 degrees.
2. Remove duck from bag. Remove giblets and neck from interior. Remove excess fat from body cavity and neck. Rinse duck inside and out under cool running water. Pat duck dry. With a sharp fork, prick the skin all over (approach at an angle) being careful not to pierce the meat (if meat is pierced, it will dry out). Carefully put the duck in the pot of boiling water; boil for 10 minutes. This will help render out some of the fat. Remove duck and let cool. Pat duck dry.

3. Mix the salt, pepper and paprika. Rub the duck inside and out with the spice mixture. Place the duck on a rack in a roasting pan breast-side up. Stuff the orange quarters, garlic and celery pieces into the cavity of the duck. Fold the neck skin under, covering the cavity. Secure with a skewer.

4. Place the roasting pan with the duck in the oven. After 15 minutes, lower the oven temperature to 350 degrees. After 45 minutes, remove duck from oven. Remove any fat that may have collected in the bottom of the roasting pan. Carefully turn duck over, place back on rack in roasting pan, and return to oven for 35 minutes. At the end of the 35 minutes, remove duck from oven, remove any fat that may have accumulated, and carefully turn duck back over so breast side faces up. Return to oven. If you have a 5-pound duck, bake for another 15 minutes. For a 6-pound duck, bake for another 20 minutes. Total cooking time should add up to 22 minutes per pound. Be careful not to overcook. The internal temperature should be 180 degrees at the thickest part of the leg and thigh joint. Remove duck from oven. Transfer duck to a cutting board and let stand 15 minutes. Remove oranges and celery from cavity and discard.

5. Carve duck and serve with Plum Sauce.

GARLIC BOK CHOY
6 servings

1 tbsp. vegetable oil
5 cloves garlic, minced
2 large shallots, minced
1/4 tsp. crushed red pepper

2 lbs. baby bok choy, quartered
2 tbsp. soy sauce
1 tsp. sesame oil

1. Add oil to a large skillet over medium-high heat. Swirl to coat the entire surface of the skillet. Add the garlic, shallots and red pepper flakes, stirring continuously for 1 to 2 minutes, or until fragrant.

2. Add the bok choy, soy sauce, and sesame oil. Toss to coat and cover. Cook for 1 to 2 minutes, uncover and toss, and then cover and continue to cook until bok choy is cooked to desired doneness (approximately 3 to 5 minutes more).

3. Serve immediately. Enjoy!

STICKY RICE
4 servings

1 cup short grain rice or sweet rice, also known as glutinous rice,
   (Sushi Rice).
1 3/4 cups water
1/2 tsp. salt

1. Mix rice and water into a medium pot. Let the rice soak for
    at least half an hour or as long as four hours.
2. Add 1/2 tsp. of salt and stir.
3. Place the pot over high heat and bring the water to a boil.
    Turn the heat to low and cover the pot, leaving the lid slight-
    ly off on one side to vent. Cook for 8 minutes, but DO NOT
    stir the rice while cooking.
4. After 8 minutes, check to see if the rice has absorbed all of
    the water by pulling the rice away from the center with a
    fork to create a hole. If there is still water, continue cooking
    for 5 to 10 minutes or until the liquid has been absorbed.
5. Remove the pot from the heat and place the lid on securely.
    Allow the rice to stand for 10 minutes before serving.

CROATIA

MENU

Pomegranate Lemon Raki

Octopus Salad

Soparnik (savory pie)

Pasticada and Gnocchi (braised beef)

Blitva (potatoes and Swiss chard)

Croatian Cheesecake

Interesting Croatian Facts:
1. Dalmatians are said to have originated in Croatia.
2. The Croatian currency, the Kuna, is named after a rodent.
3. Game of Thrones was filmed on the coast of Croatia, in Split and Dubrovnik.

POMEGRANATE LEMON RAKI
1 Serving

2 oz. raki
2 oz. pomegranate juice
1 cup ice cubes
1 cup lemon lime soda
1 lemon, sliced
Mint leaves for garnish

1. Fill a tall glass with ice cubes.
2. Add 2 oz. of raki.
3. Add one cup of lemon lime soda.
4. Pour pomegranate juice over the drink. Mix.
5. Add a slice of lemon to the rim and a sprig of mint leave to garnish.

Note: Raki is a fruit brandy. In Croatia it is generally served straight and not mixed.

OCTOPUS SALAD
4-6 Servings

1 medium or large octopus (about 5-6 lbs.), cleaned
3 lbs. waxy potatoes
1 large Spanish onion, finely sliced
2 cloves of garlic, finely sliced
Extra virgin olive oil
1 cup arugula
Salt and pepper
Parsley for garnish

1. Place the octopus and whole potatoes in a large pot filled 2/3 of the way with cold water. Add a pinch of salt.
2. Bring the water to a boil and then simmer until the potatoes are tender. Remove and drain the potatoes.
3. Continue to boil the octopus until it is tender. Add more water to keep it covered, as needed. It will take about 45-60 minutes to cook the octopus.
4. Peel potatoes and cut into medium sized chunks. Place in a large salad bowl.

5. When the octopus is cooked and tender, remove from the water and allow to cool.
6. Chop up the octopus and add to the salad bowl.
7. Add the garlic, Spanish onion, arugula, and a generous amount of olive oil.
8. Gently toss the ingredients; add salt and pepper to taste.
9. Sprinkle with parsley.

Note: We used baby octopus because that was what we had available locally; if using baby or small octopus just adjust cooking time so they do not overcook and become tough.

SOPARNIK
6 Servings

4 cups flour	1 onion, chopped
1 tsp. salt	2 tbsp. fresh parsley,
4 tbsp. canola oil	finely chopped
1 1/2 cups water	2 cloves garlic, minced
2 lbs. Swiss chard	4 tbsp. olive oil

1. Preheat oven to 350 degrees.
2. Add flour, salt, canola oil and water to a bowl and combine to prepare a firm dough.
3. Divide the dough into two balls, one slightly larger than the other. Cover with a cloth and let sit for 15 minutes.
4. Clean the Swiss chard and chop into small pieces; place in a medium bowl. Add the chopped onion and parsley to the bowl. Combine all the ingredients well.
5. Roll out the bigger piece of dough to the size of a 9" pie plate. Transfer to a baking sheet and add the chard mixture on top.
6. Roll out the smaller piece of dough and place it over the chard mixture. Press the upper dough and the lower dough together. Seal the perimeter sealing in the chard mixture.
7. Bake for 35 to 40 minutes.
8. Combine the minced garlic and the olive oil in a small bowl.
9. Remove the pie from the oven, and brush it with the garlic and olive oil mixture.
10. When cool, cut the pie into triangles to serve.

PASTICADA and GNOCCHI
4 Servings

4.5 lbs. beef, top round	1 tbsp. cloves, minced
1/2 lb. bacon	10 dried prunes, diced
1 small onion	6 dried figs
1 cup of parsley root	2 apples, peeled and quartered
3 carrots	1 1/4 cups red wine
1/2 cup celery root	2 tbsp. mustard
2 garlic cloves	3 bay leaves
2.5 tbsp. tomato paste	Small bunch of thyme
1 cup vegetable oil	Rosemary leaves
Apple cider vinegar	Salt and pepper

1. Pat the meat with a towel to dry off; make small slits with a knife, and place the bacon pieces in the slits. Salt as desired, spread mustard over the meat.
2. Place meat in a medium size bowl. Add the vegetable oil and enough apple cider vinegar to cover the meat. Let marinate for at least 5 hours, preferably overnight.
3. Brown all sides of the meat in hot oil. Remove meat from pan. Add the chopped onion, garlic, and vegetables to pan. Saute until vegetables are tender.
4. Return meat to the pan along with the red wine. Simmer covered for about two hours or until meat is tender. If needed, more wine mixed with water can be added.
5. When the meat is cooked and tender, add tomato paste, diced prunes, figs and apple quarters.
6. Cook down until all ingredients are incorporated. Add bay leaf, rosemary, thyme, and minced cloves. Salt and pepper to taste. If needed can also add a small amount of red wine to balance flavors and for proper consistency.
7. Remove the meat and cut into slices.
8. Puree the vegetables and sauce then pour over the meat to serve.
9. Serve with gnocchi and a slice of lemon.

Note: We used store brought gnocchi, but any basic gnocchi recipe will work if you prefer homemade.

BLITVA (potatoes and Swiss chard)
4 Servings

1.5 lbs. potatoes cut into 1/2 inch chunks
1 bunch Swiss chard - can substitute any firm leafy green such
  as kale or collards
1/3 cup olive oil
5 cloves garlic, sliced
Kosher salt and pepper to taste
Red pepper flakes, to taste

1. Place potatoes in a large saucepan of salted, cold water;
    water should cover the potatoes. Cook at a gentle boil until
    tender.
2. While potatoes are cooking, clean chard thoroughly, cut
    stems from leaves, cut into chunks.
3. In a large frying pan, add the olive oil and sliced garlic. Cook
    over medium heat until aromatic. Add the potatoes and
    increase heat to medium-high. Cook until potatoes begin
    to brown on the edges. Remove the potatoes and garlic,
    reserving the oil in the pan.
4. Add the Swiss chard stems to the pan and cook on medium-
    high heat; cook the stems for a minute, then add the rest
    of the Swiss chard leaves. Add salt, pepper, and red pepper
    flakes. Cook for about 3 minutes.
5. Return potatoes back to the pan to combine flavors. Taste
    for seasoning adding additional salt, pepper, red pepper
    flakes, to taste.
6. Place in serving dish.

Note: Blitva means Swiss chard in Croatian.

CROATIAN CHEESECAKE
8 Servings

Preheat oven to 325 degrees.

Crust:
2 cups graham crackers
3/4 cup almonds, sliced
3/4 cup walnuts
1/2 cup pumpkin seeds
1/3 cup wheat germ
8 tbsp. butter, salted, melted

Filling:
2 1/2 cups cottage cheese, whole milk, 4%, small curd, drained
1 cup whipped cream cheese, room temperature
3/4 cup maple sugar
4 eggs, beaten
4 tbsp. flour
1/8 tsp. salt
3 large lemons, zest and juice

Topping:
2 (6 oz.) containers Greek lemon yogurt (best is Noosa lemon
   yogurt)
3/4 cup fresh blueberries

1. Coat the bottom and sides of a 6-7" round springform pan
    with cooking spray. Cut a piece of parchment paper the size
    of the round bottom and place in the pan.
2. Pulse the graham crackers, almonds, walnuts, pumpkin
    seeds, and wheat germ in a food processor. Remove to a
    bowl. Add the melted butter and blend well.
3. Put mixture into the springform pan and pat down well,
    firming the crust. Pre-bake in the preheated 325 degrees
    oven for 6-8 minutes. Remove and let cool.
4. In a large mixing bowl, place the cottage cheese, whipped
    cream cheese, sugar, eggs, and flour. Whisk together well.
    Add the lemon juice and zest. Blend well. Pour into the pan.
5. Place the pan on a cookie sheet. Place in preheated oven,
    and bake at 325 degrees for 60-65 minutes or until a tooth-
    pick inserted in the center comes out clean. The top will
    begin to show cracks and crevices when done.
6. Place on a cooling rack. Take a butter knife and gently move

around the perimeter of the cheesecake loosening the sides.
7. When the cheesecake is cool, remove the pan.
8. Cover with plastic wrap and refrigerate for a couple of hours.
9. Before serving, spread the lemon yogurt on the top of the
    cheesecake. Place blueberries on top of the yogurt.

Note: This is more rustic and less sweet than a traditional
cheesecake.

Note: Maple sugar is a traditional sweetener used in Canada and
in the northeastern United States that is made from the sap of a
maple tree. We ordered it from Amazon.

ENGLAND

MENU

Gimlet
Prawn Cocktail
Bangers and Mash with Onion Gravy
Peas
Yorkshire Pudding
Eton Mess

Interesting English Facts:
1. French was the official language of England for over 300 years.
2. It is illegal to get drunk in English pubs.
3. England is the birthplace of William Shakespeare.

GIMLET

4 servings

2 cups Rose's Lime Juice
2 cups London's Beefeater Gin
1 lime, slice for garnish

1. Place four martini glasses in freezer. Put lime juice and gin in refrigerator. Allow all to cool.
2. Combine lime juice and gin in a pitcher. Stir to mix.
3. Pour into cold martini glasses.
4. Garnish with a slice of lime.

PRAWN COCKTAIL

4 servings

1 lb. large prawns, cooked
1 jar of cocktail sauce
Celery sticks, for garnish
Crushed ice

1. Fill four individual serving bowls half-way with ice.
2. Artfully arrange prawns on top of ice. Place a dollop of cocktail sauce atop the prawns.
3. Garnish with celery sticks.

BANGERS AND MASH

4 servings

8 high quality pork sausages
2 lbs. Yukon Gold potatoes, peeled and cut into large (2 inch) uniform chunks
1/2 tsp. salt
4 tbsp. butter
1 cup hot "whole" milk
1 batch homemade Onion Gravy (recipe follows)

1. Preheat oven to 400 degrees.
2. Place the potatoes in a pot of water and add the salt. Bring to a boil, lower the heat to a steady simmer and cook for 15 to 20 minutes or until the potatoes are just tender when pierced with a knife. Do not over boil them.
3. Thoroughly drain the potatoes and place them back in the empty pot set over very low heat to maintain warmth. Use a hand masher to mash the potatoes while they're hot.

Mash them until fluffy. Be careful not to over mash them or they will become gluey.

4. Use a spoon to stir in the butter. Once melted, stir in the hot milk gradually, allowing time for the potatoes to absorb the liquid after each addition. Add more hot milk as needed to achieve desired consistency. Season with salt and pepper to taste.

5. While the potatoes are boiling, place the sausages in a baking dish with a little oil and roast them for about 10 minutes on each side or until nicely browned.

6. To serve, place a mound of mashed potatoes on each plate, lay the sausages on the mashed potatoes and top with onion gravy. Peas are a traditional side.

Note: The term bangers supposedly originated during World War I, when meat shortages resulted in sausages being made with a number of fillers, notably water, that caused them to explode when cooked.

ONION GRAVY
10 servings

1/4 cup butter	1/2 tsp. yellow mustard
2 large yellow onions, peeled, cut in half and diced	1 tsp. salt
	1/4 tsp. pepper
2 tsp. sugar	1 tsp. Worcestershire sauce
1/2 cup red wine	1 tbsp. balsamic vinegar
2 sprigs fresh thyme	1 tbsp. cornstarch dissolved in
1 large sprig fresh sage	1 tbsp. water
2 cups beef broth	2 tbsp. cold butter

1. Melt the 1/4 cup butter in a saucepan over medium high heat. Add the diced onions and sugar. Cook for about 30 minutes until caramelized a deep golden color.

2. Add the red wine and herbs, bring to a rapid boil for 2 minutes, reduce the heat and simmer for 10 minutes.

3. Add the beef broth, mustard, salt, pepper and Worcestershire sauce, bring to a boil, reduce the heat to a low simmer and simmer covered for 20 minutes.

4. Remove sprigs of herbs. Add the vinegar, whisk in the cornstarch and simmer another minute or two until thickened, whisking continuously.

5. Add the cold butter and whisk until dissolved. Add salt and pepper to taste and more mustard, if desired.

YORKSHIRE PUDDING

12 puddings

3 large eggs
3/4 cup whole milk
3/4 cup flour
3/4 tsp. salt
1/4 cup melted butter

1. Preheat oven to 400 degrees.
2. In a medium bowl, whisk together eggs, milk, flour and salt. Do not over mix. Allow the batter to rest 30 minutes at room temperature.
3. Add a teaspoon of melted butter to each cup of a 12-cup muffin tin and transfer to the oven to heat, about 5 to 7 minutes. Once hot, divide the batter equally to fill the cups about halfway. Return the muffin tin to the oven for 10 to 12 minutes, or until the puddings are golden brown and crisp. Serve immediately.

ETON MESS

4 servings

FOR THE MERINGUE COOKIES
1 tsp. white vinegar
2 large egg whites, at room temperature
1/4 tsp. cream of tartar
Pinch of Kosher salt
1/2 cup sugar
1/2 tsp. vanilla extract

FOR THE STRAWBERRIES
1/2 lb. fresh strawberries
1 tbsp. sugar

FOR THE WHIPPED CREAM
3/4 cup heavy cream, chilled
1/2 tsp. vanilla extract
1 tbsp. powdered sugar

MERINGUE COOKIES
1. Preheat the oven to 200 degrees and place the rack in the center of the oven. Line a cookie sheet with parchment paper. Set aside.
2. Wet a paper towel with white vinegar and use it to wipe out a medium bowl to ensure there's no fat residue.

Place the egg whites in the bowl and beat with a mixer until foamy. Stir in the cream of tartar and salt.
3. Add the sugar a little at a time, beating after each addition, until soft peaks form. Add the vanilla extract and beat until the meringue holds stiff peaks.
4. Place a little of the meringue on the underside of each corner of the baking pan to hold the parchment paper flat. Using two spoons, portion the meringue into 12 mounds on the baking sheet.
5. Bake the meringue cookies for approximately 1 to 1 1/2 hours until they are pale in color and appear dry and crisp. Turn off the oven once they're done without opening the oven door and let cool completely in the oven (about 1 to 2 hours) before removing the pan.

STRAWBERRIES
1. Hull the strawberries and cut them into bite-sized chunks. Place the chunks in a small bowl, sprinkle with sugar, and toss very gently to coat. Set the bowl aside for at least 30 minutes.
2. Remove a third of the strawberries and set aside for garnish. Lightly crush the rest into a chunky compote using a wooden spoon or potato masher.

WHIPPED CREAM
1. Chill a medium bowl and mixer beaters. Pour the heavy cream into the chilled bowl and use the mixer to whip soft peaks.
2. Add the vanilla extract and powdered sugar, then beat the mixture until stiff peaks form.
3. Chill until ready to assemble.

ASSEMBLE THE DESSERT
1. Just before serving, break six meringue cookies (or more) into bite-size pieces into the whipped cream.
2. Fold in the crushed strawberries with their juices making sure not to over mix.
3. Garnish with reserved strawberries.

Note:
The generally accepted story of ETON MESS is that the strawberry, meringue and whipped cream pudding was dropped at an Eton v Harrow cricket match in the late 19th century. Rather than waste the food, it was simply scooped up off the floor and served smashed to bits in individual bowls. (Eton College is a public college in the town of Eton near Windsor in Berkshire. The founder was Henry VI in 1440.)

FIJI

MENU

Fiji Water
Fijian Passion Cocktail
Kokoda
Tamarind Shrimp
Coconut Rice
Honey Cake

Interesting Facts:
1. Fiji has 333 islands, with 223 being uninhabited
2. Cannibalism in Fiji ended in 1871.
3. The practice of walking on hot stones started in Fiji.

PASSION COCKTAIL
4 Servings

6 oz. passion fruit juice
2 oz. pineapple juice
6 oz. dark rum
6 oz. triple sec
Crushed ice
Mint to garnish

1. Combine juices, rum, and triple sec.
2. Fill blender with crushed ice.
3. Blend until slushy.
4. Serve in margarita glasses, garnished with mint.

KOKODA
4 Servings

12 oz. Mahi Mahi, boneless, skinless
3/4 cup lime juice, approx 8 limes
3/4 cup coconut milk
2 tomatoes, finely chopped
1 green pepper, finely chopped
1/3 cup red onion, finely chopped
1/2 English cucumber, finely chopped
1/3 cup parsley, chopped
1 jalapeno, finely diced
Salt and pepper, to taste

1. Cut the Mahi Mahi into cubed, bite sized pieces. Place the pieces in a bowl; cover fish completely with lime juice. Cover and place in the fridge for about six hours. The fish is cooked when the fish has turned white and opaque. Cut into one of the fish pieces to ensure it is white and opaque all the way through.
2. Add the coconut milk and the diced vegetables. Stir, then season with salt and pepper to taste.
3. Spoon into bowls or coconut halves to serve.

Note: Kokoda is traditionally served in coconut halves. The coconut halves are prepared by removing all of the coconut meat and then sanding until smooth. Wax can be applied before using. The process is simple, but labor intensive!

TAMARIND SHRIMP
4 Servings

1 oz. of fresh tamarind
5 tbsp. water
11 oz. large tiger shrimp with shell off
4 tbsp. canola oil
1 tbsp. sugar
1 tsp. sea salt
1 tbsp. soy sauce

1. Mix tamarind and water until thick and creamy. Add the shrimp and marinate for two hours.
2. Heat oil in a saucepan over medium heat. Add the shrimp and cook for one minute. Continue cooking and slowly add the sugar, salt and soy sauce.
3. When caramelized, remove from heat and place on serving dish.

COCONUT RICE
4 Servings

1 1/2 cups medium grain rice
2 1/4 cups water
2 tbsp. coconut cream
2 green onions, diced
1/2 cucumber, thinly sliced

1. Boil water in a large pot and then add the rice. Decrease the heat to medium-low and let cook for 10-15 minutes or until tender. Place on serving dish.
2. While rice is cooking, pour the coconut cream into a small saucepan and warm over low heat for five minutes. Stir continuously; do not let it boil. Remove from heat and pour over the rice. Garnish with the green onions and cucumber.

HONEY CAKE
10 Servings

1 1/4 cups all-purpose flour
1/2 cup granulated sugar
1/2 cup sour cream
1/2 cup honey
1 egg
1 tbsp. canola oil
1/2 tsp. baking soda

1/8 tsp. ground nutmeg
1/8 tsp. ground allspice
1/4 tsp. ground ginger
1/2 tsp. ground cinnamon
1 tbsp. sliced almonds
Mint

1. Preheat oven to 350 degrees.
2. Spray a 9" x 5" loaf pan with nonstick cooking spray.
3. In a large bowl, combine all the ingredients, except the almonds, and beat until well blended.
4. Pour the batter into the loaf pan and sprinkle with the almonds.
5. Bake for 45-55 minutes or until a wooden toothpick inserted in the center comes out clean.
6. Allow to cool for 10 minutes then remove from pan to a wire rack to cool.
7. When cool, slice and place on serving dish. Garnish with a sprig of mint.

HUNGARY

MENU

Budapest Cocktail
Hungarian Mushroom Soup
Chicken Paprikash with Noodles
Borsofozelek (Hungarian Style Peas)
Apple Strudel in Puff Pastry

Interesting Hungarian Facts:

1. Hungary is situated in central Europe and has the unique status of being a landlocked country entirely surrounded by other nations.
2. In Hungary, you can only name your child after there is approval from the government.

BUDAPEST COCKTAIL

4 servings

2 oz. Vodka
2 oz. Mr. Boston Wild Cherry Flavored Brandy
1 cup orange juice
Maraschino cherries and orange slice for garnish
Crushed ice

Combine liquids in a pitcher. Fill four highball glasses with crushed ice. Pour liquids into highball glasses equally. Garnish each glass with a maraschino cherry and slice of orange.

HUNGARIAN MUSHROOM SOUP

8 servings

1/2 cup butter
2 large yellow onions, chopped
2 lbs. cremini mushrooms, sliced
4 cups chicken broth
1 cup dry white wine
4 tsp. dried dill
4 tsp. minced fresh thyme
4 tsp. paprika
2 tbsp. Worcestershire
2 tsp. salt
6 tbsp. flour
2 cups whole milk
1/2 cup sour cream
2 tbsp. lemon juice, from 1 lemon
4 tbsp. fresh parsley

1. Melt butter in a large pot over medium heat. When butter is melted, add onions and mushrooms and cook, stirring occasionally, until onions are soft and translucent, about 8 minutes. Add the chicken broth, white wine, dill, thyme, paprika, Worcestershire and salt. Bring to a boil over high heat. Reduce to a simmer over low heat and cook, stirring occasionally, until the liquid reduces by 1/3, about 10 minutes or more.

2. In a small bowl, whisk flour into the milk until smooth. Add
   the milk mixture to the soup and cook, stirring occasionally,
   until the soup begins to thicken, about 10 more minutes.
3. Over low heat, slowly stir in the sour cream and lemon juice.
4. Divide the soup into bowls and top with fresh parsley to
   serve.

CHICKEN PAPRIKASH with Noodles

6 servings

6 bone-in, skin-on chicken thighs
2 tbsp. butter
1 onion, chopped
1 green bell pepper, diced
1 red bell pepper, diced
3 cloves garlic, minced
2 tbsp. tomato paste
4 tbsp. plus 1 tsp. sweet Hungarian paprika, divided
2 cups chicken broth
1/2 tsp. pepper
1 tsp. salt
3/4 cup sour cream
3 to 4 cups cooked egg noodles

1. Season the chicken thighs with salt and pepper on both
   sides.
2. Heat butter in a skillet over medium-high heat. Add chicken
   skin side down and sear undisturbed for 6 to 7 minutes.
   Flip and cook for another 3 to 4 minutes. Plate it out and
   discard the skin.
3. Discard the excess fat from the skillet leaving about a couple
   of tablespoons. Add onions and sauté onions until they start
   turning brown.
4. Add in green and red bell peppers and sauté until soft. Add
   in garlic and cook for 1 minute.
5. Stir in tomato paste and cook for 2 minutes.
6. Remove from heat and stir in 4 tbsp. sweet Hungarian
   paprika and mix well.
7. Return back to heat and add in chicken broth and cook for
   2 minutes. Add chicken thighs into the skillet and cook, covered, for 40 to 45 minutes, until chicken is fall off the bone
   tender.
8. Place sour cream in a bowl and slowly mix in a spoonful of
   the hot paprikash sauce. Do it 4 to 5 times. This ensures

the sour cream slowly comes to the temperature of the sauce and does not curdle, resulting in a smooth sauce. Mix this tempered sour cream into the skillet and mix well. Add 1 tsp. of sweet Hungarian paprika. Taste and adjust the salt and pepper.

9. Simmer on low heat for 8 to 10 minutes. Serve immediately over cooked egg noodles.

Note: We ordered the sweet Hungarian paprika from Amazon.

BORSOFOZELEK (Hungarian style peas)
6 servings

1 tbsp. olive oil
Pinch of red pepper flakes
1 cup of diced onions
2 cups frozen peas
1 cup chicken broth
1 tsp. sweet Hungarian paprika
2 tbsp. flour
1/2 cup milk
Salt, pepper and sweet Hungarian paprika, to taste

1. In a large skillet, heat olive oil with a pinch of red pepper flakes. Sauté the onions until they begin to change color.
2. Add the peas and broth. Season with salt, pepper and paprika.
3. Cook the pea mixture five minutes on medium heat.
4. Mix the flour and milk together into a slurry and stir it into the vegetables.
5. Continue to cook until the sauce thickens.
6. Adjust the seasonings to taste.

APPLE STRUDEL IN PUFF PASTRY
6 servings

3 medium Granny Smith apples, peeled, cored and diced
  1/4 inch thick
1 tsp. lemon juice, fresh
3 tbsp. flour
1/2 tsp. cinnamon
1/4 tsp. nutmeg
1/8 tsp. salt
2/3 cup dark brown sugar
1/2 cup raisins or craisins or a combination

1 sheet puff pastry
1 egg
1 tbsp. water

1. Thaw the puff pastry according to the package instructions. Make sure it's still cold when you are ready to roll it out.
2. Preheat the oven to 400 degrees. Line a baking sheet with parchment paper.
3. In a small bowl, whisk the flour, brown sugar, cinnamon, nutmeg and salt together.
4. In a large bowl, combine the apples and lemon juice. Add the flour and sugar mixture and toss to coat evenly. Add raisins or craisins.
5. On the parchment paper you prepared for the baking sheet, roll out the dough slightly about 12" x 12" using a rolling pin.
6. Using a sharp knife, cut horizontal strips about 3/4 inch wide along the pastry's left and right sides (outer thirds) of the pastry. Cut the top two and bottom two strips off and discard.
7. Spread the apple mixture down the middle one-third of the pastry lengthwise, leaving a one-inch space from the top and bottom. Fold the top and bottom strip over the apple filling.
8. Braid the pastry by folding over a strip from the left, then a strip from the right, crossing them over each other. Continue all the way down the pastry until all the strips are over the apple mixture.
9. Beat the egg with 1 tbsp. of water. Set aside.
10. Transfer the parchment with the pastry back to the baking sheet and refrigerate for 20 minutes.
11. Remove from the refrigerator and lightly brush the top and side of the pastry with the egg wash.
12. Bake for 35 to 40 minutes, until golden brown.

ICELAND

MENU

Reyka Vodka

Lobster Bisque

Rye Bread

Baked Fish

Smashed Potatoes

Blueberry Schnapps

White Chocolate Creme Brulee

Interesting Icelandic Facts:
1. There are as many as 10,000 waterfalls and roughly 130 volcanoes in Iceland.
2. More than 50 percent of Icelanders believe that elves or fairies exist.

LOBSTER BISQUE
4 servings

BISQUE
3 lobster tails (6 oz. size) or 1 lb. langoustine
2 tbsp. butter
1 tbsp. olive oil
1 onion, finely chopped
2 medium carrots, peeled and finely chopped
2 stalks celery, finely chopped
1 tsp. fresh chopped thyme
1 tsp. fresh chopped tarragon, plus more to serve
1 tsp. chicken bouillon powder
1/2 tsp. salt
1/4 tsp. black pepper
1/2 tsp. cayenne pepper
4 cloves garlic, minced
2 tbsp. tomato paste
3 tbsp. flour
1 1/4 cup dry white wine
4 cups lobster stock (recipe follows)
1 cup heavy cream

GARLIC BUTTER LOBSTER MEAT
2 tbsp. butter
2 cloves garlic, minced
Salt and pepper to taste

LOBSTER STOCK
1. Fill a large pot with 5 cups of water. Stir in 1 tsp. salt and
    bring to a boil.
2. Add lobster tails. Cover with a lid and let boil for 5 minutes
    or until bright red.
3. Remove lobster tails, reserving the liquid stock. When the
    lobsters have cooled slightly, remove the meat from the
    shells, reserving the meat and any liquid that comes out of
    the shells.
4. Return lobster shells back to the water in the pot. Bring
    to a boil, reduce heat to medium-low and let simmer for a
    further 15 minutes to draw as much flavor out of the shells
    as possible.

5. While stock is simmering, chop the meat into bite-sized piec-
    es and refrigerate.

BISQUE
1. Heat butter and oil in a large, heavy-based pot over medium
    heat. Sweat the onions, carrots, celery and fresh herbs. Cook
    until soft, about 5 minutes. Season with the bouillon pow-
    der, salt, black pepper and cayenne pepper. Stir in 4 cloves of
    minced garlic and cook until fragrant, about 1 minute.
2. Mix in tomato paste, cook for a further minute to coat vege-
    tables. Sprinkle in flour and cook, while stirring occasionally
    for a further 2 minutes.
3. Pour in wine, simmer and let reduce to half. Stir in lobster
    stock, reduce heat and gently simmer while stirring occa-
    sionally, until liquid has thickened slightly and flavors have
    blended, about 30 minutes.
4. Take off the heat, transfer mixture to a blender and blend
    until smooth. Alternatively, puree with an immersion blend-
    er until very smooth. Return to medium-low heat and stir in
    heavy cream.

GARLIC BUTTER LOBSTER MEAT
Melt butter in a skillet over medium heat. Sauté garlic for 30
seconds, until fragrant. Add in chopped lobster meat, season
with salt and pepper to taste. Lightly sauté for 1 minute while
stirring occasionally until lobster meat is just warmed through.

TO SERVE LOBSTER BISQUE
Mix 3/4 lobster meat into the bisque. Pour into individual
serving bowls. Top each bowl with remaining lobster meat and
extra tarragon.

Note:
TO REMOVE LOBSTER MEAT
Place lobster tail on your counter with the back of the tail facing
up. Use sharp kitchen shears to cut down through the center to
the end of the tail. With your thumbs and fingers, open the shell
to loosen it from the meat, opening the meat away from the
shell side walls. Pull the meat up from the bottom of the shell to
separate the shell from the meat underneath it.

BAKED FISH

6 servings

1 tbsp. butter
6 cod fillets
1 lemon
Salt and pepper to taste
1 cup Parmesan or Swiss cheese, grated
1 tbsp. mustard
1 cup cream
1/2 cup Panko breadcrumbs

1. Preheat oven to 350 degrees.
2. Butter a baking dish.
3. Put the fillets into the baking dish
4. Season the fillets with salt, pepper and freshly squeezed lemon juice.
5. Cover the fish with grated cheese.
6. Mix mustard with cream and pour it over the fillets.
7. Cover with Panko breadcrumbs.
8. Bake the fillets for 35 minutes.

SMASHED POTATOES

8 servings

2 lbs. Yukon Gold potatoes
3 tbsp. melted butter
4 cloves garlic, minced
1 tbsp. fresh chopped parsley
Salt and black pepper to taste
A light spray of olive oil
3 tbsp. Parmesan cheese (or more)

1. Preheat oven to broil on medium-high heat (400 degrees).
2. Place potatoes in a large pot of salted water. Bring to a boil; cook 15 to 20 minutes or until just fork-tender. Drain well.
3. Lightly grease a large baking sheet with cooking oil spray. Arrange potatoes on the sheet and use a potato masher to LIGHTLY flatten each potato in one piece. Do not press too hard, or the potatoes will end up mashed.
4. Mix together the butter, garlic and parsley. Pour the mixture over each potato. Sprinkle with salt and pepper. Spray lightly with olive oil.

5. Broil until they are golden and crispy (about 10 to 15 minutes). Remove from the oven, sprinkle over the Parmesan cheese and return to the oven until the cheese is melted.

BLUEBERRY SCHNAPPS
4 servings

1 cup pureed blueberries
2 cups of water
1/2 cup sugar
1/2 cup vodka

1. Cook together the sugar, water and blueberry puree until the sugar is melted and syrup is slightly thickened. Cool and add the vodka. Freeze.
2. Just before serving, puree the frozen schnapps in a blender to a slushy consistency and serve on the side with the White Chocolate Creme Brulee (recipe follows).

WHITE CHOCOLATE CREME BRULEE
Serves 4

Custard Ingredients:
1 cup heavy cream
1 cup Skyr (You can substitute 1 cup heavy cream if you cannot find Skyr. See note.)
1/4 cup plus 3 tbsp. sugar
1/2 cup white chocolate chips, chopped
5 large egg yolks

Brulee Ingredient:
4 tbsp. sugar

1. Preheat oven to 250 degrees.
2. Heat cream, Skyr and 1/4 cup sugar in a small saucepan over medium heat, stirring until the sugar dissolves and the cream just begins to simmer. Add chocolate and whisk until melted and smooth.
3. Whisk the 3 tbsp. sugar with the egg yolks in a medium bowl. Slowly pour cream mixture into yolk mixture whisking constantly.
4. Pour custard mixture into 4 six-ounce ramekins. Transfer ramekins to a roasting pan and fill pan with enough hot water to reach halfway up the sides of the ramekins. Bake until custard is set, about 1 hour to 1 hour and 15 minutes. Carefully remove the ramekins and let them cool.

5. Refrigerate the custard for at least one hour. They can be
    made up to a day ahead of time.
6. Remove from refrigerator and top each ramekin with one
    tbsp. of sugar. Gently shake each ramekin to coat the top
    evenly with the sugar.
7. Use a kitchen torch to caramelize the sugar.

Note: Skyr is an Icelandic dairy product and has the consistency
of yogurt.

IRELAND

MENU

Guinness
Guinness and Cheddar Fondue with
Bread, Apples and Brats to dip
Irish Beef Stew
Irish Soda Bread
Irish Apple Crumble with Whiskey Cream
Jameson Irish Whiskey

Interesting Irish Facts:

1. In 1759 Arthur Guinness signed a 9,000-year lease on property which is now home to the Guinness Storehouse in the heart of Dublin.
2. Ireland has the largest number of redheads in the world.
3. The Titanic was built in Belfast, Ireland.

GUINNESS AND CHEDDAR FONDUE
8 servings

3 cups sharp cheddar cheese, grated
1/4 cup flour
1/4 tsp. cayenne
1/8 tsp. nutmeg
1/4 tsp. allspice
One can of Guinness–14.9 oz.
4 tbsp. butter
1 tbsp. Dijon mustard
2 tsp. Worcestershire

1. In a large bowl place grated cheddar cheese. Add flour, cayenne, nutmeg, and allspice. Mix well to coat the cheese.
2. Place a medium pot on the stove and heat to medium. Pour in the Guinness and add the butter. When the butter is melted, stir in the mustard.
3. Slowly begin adding the cheese mixture in 1/4 cup increments stirring constantly to melt the cheese into the beer and butter mixture. When you have completed adding the cheese, add the Worcestershire and stir quickly. Remove from heat.
4. Pour the mixture into a fondue pot. Keep the heat on low beneath the fondue pot.
5. Serve with bread cubes, sliced apples and slices of brats.

IRISH BEEF STEW
12 servings

8 slices of bacon, diced
1/3 cup flour
1 tsp. salt
1/2 tsp. pepper
3 lbs. beef stew meat, cut into 1-inch cubes
1 lb. whole fresh mushrooms, washed and quartered
3 medium onions, chopped
2 medium carrots, chopped

1/4 cup celery, chopped
1 tbsp. oil
2 tsp. garlic, minced
1 tbsp. tomato paste
4 cups beef broth
1 cup Guinness
2 bay leaves
1 tsp. dried thyme
1 tsp. dried parsley flakes
2 tsp. salt
1 tsp. dried rosemary
2 lbs. Yukon Gold potatoes, cut into 1-inch cubes
2 tbsp. cornstarch
2 tbsp. cold water
1 cup frozen peas

1. In a stockpot, cook bacon over medium heat until crisp.
    Using a slotted spoon, remove to paper towels. In a large
    shallow dish, combine flour, 1 tsp. salt and 1/2 tsp. pepper.
    Add beef a few pieces at a time and coat thoroughly. Brown
    beef in the bacon drippings. Remove and set aside.
2. In the same pot, sauté the mushrooms, onions, carrots and
    celery in oil until tender. Add the garlic and cook 1 minute
    longer. Stir in the tomato paste until blended. Add the
    broth, beer, bay leaves, thyme, parsley, rosemary and 2 tsp.
    salt. Return the beef and the bacon to the pot. Bring to a
    boil. Reduce heat; cover and simmer until the beef is tender,
    approximately 2 hours.
3. Add the potatoes. Return to a boil. Reduce heat; cover
    and simmer until potatoes are tender, about 1 hour longer.
    Combine cornstarch and water until smooth; stir into the
    stew. Bring to a boil; cook and stir until thickened, about 2
    minutes. Add peas; heat through. Discard the bay leaves.
4. Enjoy with some Irish Soda Bread and more Guinness!!!

IRISH SODA BREAD
6 servings

3 cups flour
2/3 cup sugar
3 tsp. baking powder
1 tsp. salt
1 tsp. baking soda
1 cup raisins

2 large eggs, room temperature, beaten
1 1/2 cups buttermilk
1 tbsp. canola oil

1. Preheat oven to 350 degrees. In a large bowl, combine flour,
    sugar, baking powder, salt and baking soda. Stir in raisins.
2. In a small bowl, measure out 1 tbsp. of the beaten eggs.
    Reserve for later.
3. In a medium bowl, combine buttermilk, oil and remaining
    eggs. Stir into the flour mixture just until moistened. The
    dough will be sticky.
4. Transfer to a greased 9 inch round baking pan. Brush with
    reserved egg.
5. Bake 45 to 50 minutes or until a toothpick inserted in the
    center comes out clean. Cool 10 minutes before removing
    from pan to a wire rack to cool. Cut into wedges.

IRISH APPLE CRUMBLE WITH WHISKEY CREAM
8 servings

For the Apple Crumble:
3 1/2 lbs. of apples (Granny Smith and Honeycrisp)
1/2 lemon, juiced
1 tsp. cinnamon
1 tsp. allspice
1 tbsp. flour
1/3 cup sugar
1 cup flour
1 cup rolled oats
2/3 cup brown sugar
1/2 cup butter, softened
1 tbsp. cinnamon
1 tsp. allspice
1/8 tsp. salt

1. Preheat the oven to 375 degrees.
2. Peel and core the apples. Cut the apples into 1/4 inch slices.
    Place them in a large mixing bowl. Add the juice of 1/2
    lemon, 1 tsp. cinnamon, 1 tsp. allspice, 1 tbsp. flour and 1/3
    cup sugar. Mix to combine and set aside.
3. In a medium mixing bowl, combine 1 cup flour, 1 cup oats,
    2/3 cup brown sugar, 1 tbsp. cinnamon, 1 tsp. allspice and 1/8
    tsp. salt. Stir to combine. Add in softened butter. Mix until
    you have a soft "crumble" texture.

4. Grease and flour a 9 x 13 inch baking pan. Pour in the apple mixture. Sprinkle the "crumble" in an even layer over the top.
5. Bake at 375 degrees for 40 minutes or until golden brown.

1 1/2 cup heavy whipping cream
1/3 cup powdered sugar
1/4 cup Jameson Whiskey

1. Combine whipping cream and powdered sugar in the bowl of a mixer. Whisk until soft mounds form. You do not want stiff peaks for this recipe. The cream should be thick but still pourable.
2. Add the whiskey and fold to combine.
3. Serve the Apple Crumble with a large dollop of Whiskey Cream!

JAMAICA

MENU

Rum Punch
Stamp and Go (fish fritters)
Jerk Chicken
Rice and Peas
Jamaican Carrots
Rum Cake

Interesting Jamaican Facts:

1. Ian Fleming wrote all his James Bond thrillers in Jamaica at his home, GoldenEye.
2. Jamaica sits on top of a large underwater mountain.
3. Jamaica is home to one of the largest butterflies in the world – grows up to 3" in length, avg. wingspan of 6"!

RUM PUNCH
6 servings

2 1/2 cups pineapple juice
2 1/2 cups orange juice
1 cup 151 proof rum
1/2 cup dark rum
1/4 cup coconut
  flavored rum

1/4 cup fresh lime juice
3 tbsp. grenadine syrup
1 orange, sliced
1 lime, sliced
1 lemon, sliced

1. Gather all ingredients.
2. Stir pineapple juice, orange juice, 151 proof rum, dark rum, coconut flavored rum, lime juice, and grenadine syrup together in a punch bowl.
3. Float orange slices, lime slices and lemon slices in the punch.
4. Ladle the punch into ice filled glasses. Garnish with lime slice on rim of glass.

STAMP and GO (fish fritters)
8 servings

6 oz. dried salted cod
Cold water, to cover
1 cup all-purpose flour
2 tsp. ground black pepper

1 tsp. baking powder
2 green onions, chopped
1/2 cup water
Vegetable oil for frying

1. Soak cod in cold water to rehydrate it and remove excess salt, 8 hour minimum.
2. Remove bones and skin from fish. Flake and shred fish into small pieces; set aside.
3. Sift flour, pepper, and baking powder into a large bowl. Add green onions and flaked cod. Pour in 1/2 cup water (can add a small amount more water if batter is too thick), stir until well blended.
4. Heat 1/4 inch of oil in a large cast iron skillet over medium heat.
5. Drop rounded spoonfuls of batter into the skillet; fry in hot oil until golden brown and crisp, about 5 minutes per side. Drain on paper towels and serve hot.

Note: I did not use dried salted cod but made a quick salted cod.

To make salted cod:

Place fish fillets in a large pot. Add water to cover fish and bring to a boil for 10 minutes (more or less, depending on thickness of filets). Drain off water and allow the fish to cool. Using two forks flake the fish and then sprinkle with salt to taste.

JERK CHICKEN
10 servings

1 medium onion, coarsely diced
3 medium scallions, chopped
2 scotch bonnet chiles, chopped
2 garlic cloves, finely chopped
1 tbsp. five-spice powder
1 tbsp. allspice berries, coarsely ground
1 tbsp. coarsely ground black pepper
1 tsp. dried thyme
1 tsp. freshly grated nutmeg
1 tsp. kosher salt
1/2 cup soy sauce
1 tbsp. vegetable oil
2 chickens, quartered

1. In a food processor, combine the onion, scallions, chiles, garlic, five-spice powder, allspice, pepper, thyme, nutmeg, and salt; process to a coarse paste. While processing, add the soy sauce and oil in a steady stream. Place chicken and marinade in a shallow dish; make sure the chicken is thoroughly covered with the marinade. Cover and refrigerate overnight.
2. Remove the chicken from the refrigerator and bring to room temperature. Grill the chicken over a medium-hot fire until well browned on both sides and cooked through (35-40 minutes). Transfer the chicken to a platter and serve.

RICE and PEAS
8 servings

1/2 cup dry red kidney beans
2 garlic cloves, crushed
5 allspice berries
1 tsp. ginger
1 tsp. salt
4 1/2 - 5 cups water
1 cup coconut milk
4 sprigs of thyme
1 scallion diced
1/2 red onion, diced
1 scotch bonnet pepper
1 1/4 cup long grain rice

1. Place kidney beans, garlic, allspice berries, ginger and salt in instant pot. Add 4 1/2 to 5 cups of water and cook for 20 minutes on high pressure, then release pressure.

2. Once the beans are cooked and tender, add the coconut milk, thyme, scallion, onion, and a whole scotch bonnet pepper. Cover the pot and bring it to a boil. Taste and adjust seasoning as needed.
3. Rinse rice and add to beans mixture. Place lid on pot and bring to a boil. Turn to low and let the rice steam until all the liquid evaporates. Turn off and let the rice sit for another 3 - 5 minutes.
4. Remove the thyme stems, allspice berries and scotch bonnet pepper.

Note: Yes, it is suppose to be rice and peas. For some unknown reason, in Jamaica red kidney beans are called peas.

JAMAICAN CARROTS
Servings 4

1 lb. carrots, peeled and sliced	1 tsp. pineapple juice
1 tbsp. butter	1 tsp. ground cumin
2 tbsp. brown sugar	2 garlic cloves, minced
1 tsp. hot sauce	1/4 tsp. chili powder
1 tsp. fresh lemon juice	Salt to taste

1. In a medium saucepan, add the carrots and cover with water; bring to a boil over medium high heat. Cook, stirring occasionally, for 10 minutes, or until the carrots are fork-tender; drain and place in a medium bowl.
2. In the same saucepan, over medium heat, melt the butter. Add the brown sugar, hot sauce, lemon juice, pineapple juice, cumin, garlic, and chili powder.
3. Cook, stirring, for 2 to 3 minutes, or until the sugar bubbles and the spices are fragrant.
4. Pour the sauce over the carrots and toss to coat.
5. Salt to taste; serve.

RUM CAKE
Servings 16

Cake ingredients:	1/2 cup soft butter
2 1/4 cups flour	1/4 cup vegetable oil
1/4 cup cornstarch	1/2 cup evaporated milk
3 tsp. baking powder	4 eggs
1/2 tsp. salt	1 tbsp. vanilla extract
1 1/4 cups sugar	1/3 cup rum

Rum and butter syrup ingredients:
1/4 cup butter
1/2 cup sugar
1/4 cup water
1/2 - 3/4 cup rum
1/2 tsp. vanilla extract

1. Preheat oven to 325 degrees. Grease and flour bundt cake pan.
2. Place flour, cornstarch, baking powder, salt, sugar, butter and oil in a medium bowl. Mix on low speed until the butter and oil are well incorporated.
3. Mix in the milk. Add the eggs one at a time; scrape the sides and bottom of the bowl well after each egg is added.
4. Mix in the rum and vanilla extract until the batter is smooth.
5. Pour the batter into the prepared pan and bake for 55-65 minutes or until a wooden toothpick inserted into the center comes out clean.
6. Cool the cake on a wire rack after removing from the pan.

Rum and butter syrup
1. Place the butter, water, and sugar in a small saucepan.
2. Bring to a slow boil and simmer for 7-8 minutes.
3. Remove from the heat and allow to cool completely before adding in the rum and vanilla extract.

Adding syrup to the cake
1. Place the cooled cake back in the bundt pan. This will catch any syrup that drips.
2. With a long skewer, poke holes from the top all the way through to the bottom of the cake.
3. Spoon the rum and butter syrup over the top of the cake.
4. Cover with plastic wrap and let set for at least several hours.
5. Place on cake plate to serve.

Note: I put flaked coconut on the top of the cake for decoration. I served it with a slice of pineapple and a dollop of whip cream on the side.

LAOS

MENU

Lost in Laos
Ginger and Lemongrass Iced Tea
Shrimp Larb
Mok Pa (steamed fish)
Luang Prabang Salad
Nam Van Sul Lee (sweet corn and
coconut pudding)

Interesting Laotian Facts:

1. Buddhism is the largest religion.
2. Laos is the only landlocked country in Southeast Asia.
3. Coffee is Laos' largest agricultural export. A traditional Laotian iced coffee, sold at street stalls, is served in a plastic bag with a large dollop of condensed milk at the bottom, lots of ice, and a straw to drink it from the bag.

LOST IN LAOS
2 servings

2 oz. gin
1/2 oz. Green Chartreuse
2 oz. fresh coconut milk
3/4 oz. fresh lime juice
1/2 oz. agave syrup
1/4 oz. fresh turmeric
Lime slice for garnish
Ice

1. In a shaker, muddle the lime juice, agave, Chartreuse, turmeric and one slice of lime.
2. Add the gin, coconut milk, and ice.
3. Shake, then strain into a glass filled with ice.
4. Garnish with a lime slice on the rim of the glass.

GINGER AND LEMONGRASS ICED TEA

8 servings

1/2 cup sugar
7 1/2 cups water, divided
1 large stalk lemongrass, dry tops and tough outer leaves
   removed, cut into small rounds (about 1/4 cup)
1" x 2" piece of ginger, peeled and chopped (about 2 tbsp.)
4 mild black tea bags
Ice

1. In a small saucepan, combine the sugar, 1/2 cup of the water, lemongrass, and ginger. Bring to a boil over medium-high heat, stirring to dissolve the sugar. Reduce heat to low and simmer for 2 minutes. Remove from heat and allow the lemongrass and ginger to steep in the syrup for at least half an hour.
2. Bring 4 cups of water to a boil. Turn off the heat and add the teabags; allow to steep for 5 minutes. Remove the tea bags and pour into a heat-proof pitcher.
3. Strain the lemongrass ginger syrup through a small sieve. Add the strained syrup to the pitcher of tea. Add three cups of cold water to the tea and stir well. Chill the tea and serve over ice.

SHRIMP LARB
6 Servings

1/4 cup sweet white rice (sometimes labeled glutinous)
2 tbsp. unseasoned rice vinegar
1/4 cup fresh lime juice
1/4 cup fish sauce
2 tbsp. minced lemongrass, plus 1/3 cup thinly sliced rounds
  (approx 4 stalks)
1 piece ginger (1 inch), peeled and minced (about 2 tbsp.); plus a
  4" piece, peeled, and sliced into thin matchsticks (1/2 cup)
2 tbsp. minced shallot, plus 3/4 cup thinly sliced rounds (approx.
  5 shallots)
1/4 cup sugar
2 Thai chili peppers, sliced into thin rounds
2 tbsp. vegetable oil, plus more for frying
Salt
1 1/2 lbs. of shrimp, peeled, deveined, and coarsely chopped
1/2 cup unsalted roasted peanuts, plus more for serving
1/4 cup sliced fresh mint leaves, plus whole leaves for serving
1/4 cup fresh basil leaves, plus whole leaves for serving
1 head butter lettuce, leaves separated
1 English cucumber, sliced into 1/4" rounds

1. Toast rice in a small skillet over medium heat, shaking pan
    frequently, until golden brown, about 10 minutes. Let cool
    slightly, then grind to a powder using a mortar and pestle or
    spice grinder.
2. Combine vinegar, 2 tbsp. lime juice, fish sauce, minced
    lemongrass, ginger, and shallot.
3. Heat sugar in a covered small saucepan over medium-
    low heat until it melts, about 5 minutes. Remove lid and
    continue cooking, swirling pan until sugar is deep amber.
    Remove from heat.
4. Carefully add vinegar mixture (mixture will bubble and
    harden). Return to medium heat, stirring until sugar
    dissolves again. Remove from heat; stir in remaining 2 tbsp.
    lime juice and peppers. Let cool completely.
5. Heat 1/4 inch oil in skillet over medium heat. Add
    lemongrass rounds and cook, stirring occasionally with
    a fork, until golden, about two minutes. Transfer to a
    paper towel lined plate and sprinkle with salt. Fry ginger
    matchsticks and 1/2 cup shallot rounds in separate batches
    in same manner.
6. Season shrimp with 1/2 tsp. salt. Heat a large skillet over

medium-high heat. Add 2 tbsp. oil. Add remaining 1/4 cup shallot rounds; cook until soft and golden in places, 2 to 3 minutes. Add shrimp and cook, stirring frequently, until opaque, 2 to 3 minutes. Transfer to a bowl and toss with vinegar mixture and rice powder. Refrigerate at least one hour and up to one day.
7.   When ready to serve, stir in peanuts and sliced mint and basil. Spoon into lettuce leaves with cucumber. Top with whole herbs, fried aromatics, and more peanuts.

MOK PA (steamed fish)
4 Servings

4 fillets white fish, boned, skinless, and diced
1 piece lemongrass (about 2 inches) sliced and chopped small
2 kaffir lime leaves, finely sliced
2-3 cloves garlic, chopped
2 shallots, chopped
1 piece ginger (about 1/2 inch) peeled and finely chopped
1 Thai chili
1 tsp. sticky rice powder or glutinous rice flour
1 tbsp. fish sauce or anchovy paste
1 egg
1/2 cup fresh dill, chopped
1-2 green onions, chopped
Handful of Thai basil leaves
4 sheets of parchment paper

1.   Grind the chopped lemongrass, kaffir lime leaves, garlic, shallots, ginger, and Thai chili with a mortar and pestle until a smooth paste.
2.   Place fish into a mixing bowl; add the herb paste, sticky rice powder, fish sauce and egg. Mix well.
3.   Add the dill, green onion, and basil. Mix until well combined.
4.   Lay out one piece of the parchment paper.
5.   Place a ladle full of the fish mixture in the center of the paper. Fold up ends; then wrap sides around. Secure with wooden toothpicks or skewers.
6.   Place parcels into a steamer. Cover and steam for 30 minutes. If you do not have a steamer, it can be cooked on a cookie sheet in the oven at 350 degrees.
7.   Serve with sticky rice.

Note: If cooking in the oven, soak wooden toothpicks or wooden skewers in water first so they will not burn.

LUANG PRABANG SALAD
6 Servings

1 head green lettuce, chopped
2 oz. watercress, chopped
1/2 cup cilantro, torn
1/2 cup mint leaves, torn
1/3 cup dill, torn
2 tomatoes, sliced
1 cucumber, sliced
4 hard-boiled eggs, sliced
1/4 cup chopped peanuts
3 green onions, chopped
For the dressing:
1 tbsp. fish sauce
2 limes, juiced
2 tbsp. sugar
1 hard-boiled egg
3 hard-boiled egg yolks

For the salad:
1. Toss together lettuce, watercress, cilantro, mint and dill.
    Add tomatoes, cucumbers and sliced eggs.
2. Top with peanuts and green onions.

For the dressing:
1. Blend all ingredients together in a blender until creamy.
2. Drizzle over salad.

NAM VAN SUL LEE (sweet corn and coconut pudding)
6 Servings

2 1/4 cups of water, divided
1/2 cup of tapioca pearls
Pinch of salt
1/2 cup of sugar
1 - 14 oz. can of full fat coconut milk/cream
4 cups of fresh sweet corn kernels, sliced thin (approx 4 ears
   of corn)

1. In a small bowl, pour enough of the water over tapioca
    pearls to submerge under 1 inch of water, for approximately
    five minutes to soften them. Drain and set aside.
2. Boil the remaining water in a small saucepan.
3. Add the thinly sliced corn and salt to the boiling water.

Simmer for 3-5 minutes until the corn is tender.
4. Add in tapioca pearls. Bring to a boil and boil for another 3 minutes.
5. Slowly pour and stir in coconut milk and sugar to fully incorporate the ingredients. The tapioca pearls will become translucent.
6. Simmer for approximately 5-10 minutes until the mixture has a smooth, pudding texture.
7. Remove from heat to cool and refrigerate for an hour before serving.
8. Serve with whipped cream.

RUSSIA

MENU

St. Petersburg Vodka
Herring on Toast Points
Beef and Beet Borscht
Classic Beef Stroganoff
Russian Tea Cakes
Salted Caramel White Russians

Interesting Russian Facts:

1. Russia is the world's largest country, occupying one-tenth of all the land on earth.
2. Russia is home to the longest railway in the world, the Trans-Siberian Railroad.
3. It would take you six years to see everything in the Hermitage Museum in St. Petersburg if you spent two minutes at each exhibit.

R E C I P E S

HERRING ON TOAST POINTS

4 servings

1 small jar pickled herring
6 slices of good-quality white bread
2 tbsp. butter, melted
Salt, to taste
Freshly ground black pepper, to taste

1. Heat the broiler to 500 degrees or High and position the top rack about 6 inches from the heat source.
2. Using a serrated knife, cut off the crusts from each slice of bread. Discard the crusts.
3. Slice each piece into 2 triangles.
4. Arrange the bread on a large baking sheet.
5. Brush the top of each piece of bread with the melted butter, then sprinkle the slices lightly with salt and pepper.
6. Broil for about 1 1/2 minutes on the buttered side, or until gold brown. Flip and brown the other side for about 1 1/2 minutes. Allow to cool slightly.
7. Place a dollop of herring on top of each toast point. Enjoy!

BEEF AND BEET BORSCHT

8 servings

1 (1 inch thick) slice bone-in beef shank
3 qts. water
1 onion, chopped
1 cup chopped carrots
1/2 cup chopped celery
1 bay leaf
3 cups peeled and diced beets
2 cups chopped cabbage
1/4 cup white vinegar, or to taste
Salt and pepper, to taste
1 cup sour cream, for garnish
2 tbsp. chopped fresh dill, for garnish

1. Cook beef shank in a large soup pot over high heat until browned, about 3 minutes per side; add water, onion, carrots, celery and bay leaf to the pot. Bring to a simmer and cook until meat is tender and falling off the bone, about 4 hours. Strain broth and discard all solids, including the beef shank.

2. Combine beef broth, beets and cabbage in a large soup pot; cook, stirring occasionally, until beets are tender, about 30 minutes. Reduce heat to low; add vinegar, salt and black pepper.
3. Serve garnished with sour cream and dill.

CLASSIC BEEF STROGANOFF
4 servings

1 lb. beef tenderloin or sirloin steak, about 1/2 inch thick
2 tbsp. butter
1/2 lb. mushrooms, washed, trimmed and sliced
1 medium onion, minced
1 can (10 1/2 oz.) condensed beef broth
2 tbsp. catsup
1 clove garlic, minced
1 tsp. salt
3 tbsp. flour
1 cup sour cream
3 to 4 cups hot cooked egg noodles

1. Cut meat across the grain into 1/2 inch strips, about 1 1/2 inches long.
2. Melt butter in large skillet. Add mushrooms and onions, cook and stir until onion is tender, then remove from skillet.
3. In the same skillet, cook meat until light brown. Reserving 1/3 cup of the broth, stir in remaining broth, the catsup, garlic and salt. Cover; simmer 15 minutes.
4. Blend reserved broth and flour; stir into meat mixture. Add mushrooms and onion.
5. Heat to boiling, stirring constantly. Boil and stir 1 minute. Reduce heat. Stir in sour cream, heat. Serve over noodles.

RUSSIAN TEA CAKES
3 dozen

1 cup butter
1 tsp. vanilla extract
6 tbsp. confectioners sugar
2 cups flour
1 cup chopped walnuts
1/2 cup confectioners sugar (or more) for decoration

1. Preheat oven to 350 degrees.
2. In a medium bowl, cream butter and vanilla until smooth. Combine the 6 tbsps. confectioners sugar and flour; stir into

the butter mixture until just blended. Mix in the chopped
    walnuts.
3. Roll dough into 1 inch balls, and place them 2 inches apart
    on an ungreased cookie sheet.
4. Bake for 12 minutes in the preheated oven. When cool, roll
    in remaining confectioners sugar. I usually roll mine in the
    sugar a second or even a third time.

SALTED CARAMEL WHITE RUSSIANS
4 servings

4 tbsp. caramel ice cream topping
8 oz. Kahlua
8 oz. vodka
8 oz. heavy cream
Flake sea salt for garnish
Crushed ice

1. Drizzle caramel around the sides and in the bottom of each
    of four highball glasses.
2. Add 2 oz. of Kahlua and 2 oz. of vodka to each glass.
3. Add ice and drizzle 2 oz. of cream to each glass.
4. Add a pinch or two of flaked sea salt.
5. Serve immediately.

U S A
SOUTH CAROLINA

MENU

Bourbon Sweet Tea Cocktail
Carolina Cowboy Dip and Chips
Low Country Boil
Hush Puppies
Huguenot Torte

Interesting South Carolinian Facts:

1. Just outside of Charleston is one of the country's oldest living trees, The Angel Oak. It is estimated to be at least 500 years old.
2. On Morgan Island's 2,000 acres of land roam a colony of more than 3,000 rhesus monkeys.
3. Edgar Allen Poe was stationed at Fort Moultrie on Sullivan's Island. He was only 18 when he enlisted, but said he was 22, and enlisted under an assumed name, Edgar A. Perry.

BOURBON SWEET TEA COCKTAIL
6 Servings

7 cups water, divided
6 black tea bags
1 cup white sugar
1 inch ginger, peeled
1/2 cup lemon juice
3/4 cup bourbon
12 dashes bitters
Ice
Lemon slices
Fresh mint

1. Bring 6 cups of water to a boil. Add tea bags and brew 3-4 minutes.
2. Remove tea bags.
3. While tea is brewing, combine one cup water, sugar, ginger, and lemon juice in a small saucepan. Bring to a simmer; stir until sugar is completely dissolved. Pour syrup through a fine strainer to remove any pieces of ginger or lemon pulp.
4. Combine tea and simple syrup; adjusting the amount of syrup to taste depending on level of sweetness desired.
5. Stir in bourbon and bitters.
6. Serve over ice with lemon slices and fresh mint for garnish.

CAROLINA COWBOY DIP AND CHIPS
12 Servings

15 oz. can sweet yellow corn, drained and rinsed
15 oz. can black-eyed peas, drained and rinsed
15 oz. can black beans, drained and rinsed
1/2 cup minced red onion
1 1/2 cups finely diced celery
4 oz. can diced green chiles
1/4 cup olive oil
1/2 cup apple cider vinegar
3/4 cup sugar
1/4 cup water

1. Drain and rinse the beans and corn.
2. Finely dice the celery.

3.   Finely mince the red onion.
4.   Whisk together the olive oil, water, apple cider vinegar, and sugar.
5.   In a large bowl, mix together the beans, peas, corn, celery, and red onion. Add the diced green chiles. Pour in the marinade and mix well.
6.   Refrigerate for at least four hours. Strain off excess liquid before serving.
7.   Serve with tortilla chips.

LOW COUNTRY BOIL

8 Servings

16 small potatoes
8 ears of corn, shucked and broken in half
4 onions, peeled and cut in half
2 kielbasa sausages cut into 1 1/2 inch pieces
2 fresh lemons cut in half
1/2 - 1 cup Old Bay Seasoning
2 lbs. frozen easy peel shrimp

1.   Fill large stock pot with enough water to cover all ingredients.
2.   Add Old Bay Seasoning, lemon halves, potatoes and onions.
3.   Bring to a boil and cook for 10 minutes.
4.   Add sausage pieces and cook another 5 minutes.
5.   Add corn and boil another 10 minutes.
6.   Add frozen shrimp and cook 3-5 minutes or until shrimp are pink.
7.   Drain liquid from pot.
8.   Serve while hot with cocktail sauce and melted butter for dipping. Add additional Old Bay Seasoning to taste.

Note: A Low Country Boil is traditionally served dumped onto a table covered with newspaper. We used parchment paper with a newsprint design that we found on Amazon.

HUSH PUPPIES

8 Servings

1/2 cup all purpose flour
1/2 cup yellow cornmeal
1/2 tsp. salt
1/4 tsp. baking soda
1/2 tsp. freshly ground pepper
1 large egg

1/2 cup buttermilk
1 cup minced onion
2 cups vegetable oil

1. Place flour, cornmeal, salt, baking soda, and pepper in a
   bowl. Mix well and then make a well in the center of the
   mixture.
2. In a small bowl beat the egg and buttermilk with a fork until
   combined.
3. Add mixture to well in dry ingredients. Stir until moistened.
   Stir in onion.
4. Pour oil into 10 inch cast iron skillet and heat to 375 degrees.
   Drop batter by tablespoonful into oil and fry in batches for 3
   minutes on each side until golden.
5. Drain on paper towels. Best if served immediately.

HUGUENOT TORTE

12 Servings

2 large eggs
1 1/3 cups granulated sugar
1/4 cup all-purpose flour
2 1/2 tsp. baking powder
1/2 tsp. cinnamon
1/4 tsp. salt
1 large green apple peeled, cored, and diced
1 1/4 cups chopped pecans, divided
1 1/2 tsp. vanilla extract

1. Preheat oven to 325 degrees.
2. Spray a 9" square baking pan with non-stick baking spray.
3. Beat eggs for 2-3 minutes with an electric mixer on medium-
   high or until eggs are frothy and light yellow in color.
4. Add sugar, flour, baking powder, cinnamon, salt, apples, 1 cup of
   chopped pecans and vanilla extract; mix until just combined.
5. Pour mixture into prepared baking pan.
6. Bake for 40-45 minutes, or until the top is golden brown
   and crusty. Sprinkle with remaining pecans.
7. Let cool before serving. Usually served with whipped cream,
   but I served it with vanilla ice cream.

Note: Huegenot Torte is not a true torte. The recipe was first
printed in 1950 in a community cookbook. The recipe was based
on Ozark pudding and was named for the Huguenot Tavern,
a Charleston restaurant where the developer of the dessert
worked. It is now an iconic Charleston dessert.